KANJI
STARTER 1

KANJI
STARTER 1

Daiki Kusuya

Stone Bridge Press • Berkeley, California

Published by
Stone Bridge Press
P.O. Box 8208
Berkeley, CA 94707
TEL 510-524-8732 • sbp@stonebridge.com • www.stonebridge.com

First published by ICG Muse, Inc., New York and Tokyo. Reprinted by permission of IBC Publishing, Tokyo.

Printed in the United States of America.

2011 2010 2009 2008 2007 2006   10 9 8 7 6 5 4 3 2 1

CONTENTS

PREFACE

There are about 8,000 to 10,000 kanji character entries in a general kanji dictionary. About 2,000 of these characters are designated as "daily-use" kanji by the Japanese government.

Of these 2,000 characters, some can be easily understood by the use of pictographs; this book contains about 200 such characters.

Most of the pictographs in this book are based on their historical development, but some are not (I created them). The goal is to teach the meanings of kanji characters, not to show how they were derived.

DAIKI KUSUYA

SECTION 1

NOTE:

One kanji character may be pronounced in different ways depending on how it is used. In SECTION 1 and SECTION 2, the pronunciation shown along with each character is only one of the possible ways to pronounce it.

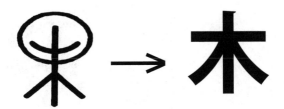 木

TREE

[ki]

WOODS

[hayashi]

森

FOREST

[mori]

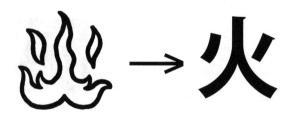 火

FIRE

[hi]

BLAZE

[honō]

ASH

[hai]

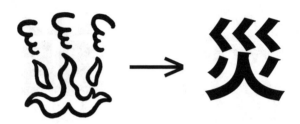

DISASTER

[wazawa-i]

MOUNTAIN

[yama]

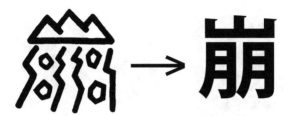

landslide

COLLAPSE

[kuzu-reru]

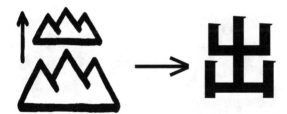

mountain
over mountain

**PROTRUDE, GO
OUT**

[de-ru]

15

HILL
[oka]

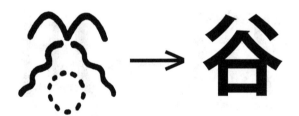

area between
mountains

VALLEY
[tani]

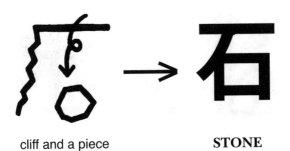

cliff and a piece

STONE

[ishi]

→ 川

RIVER

[kawa]

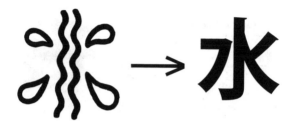

WATER

[mizu]

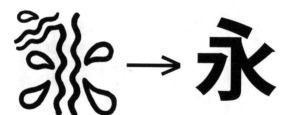

stream having
a branch,
i.e. a long stream

**LONG,
ETERNAL**

[naga-i]

ICE

[kōri]

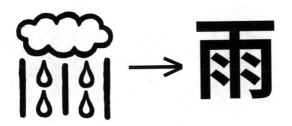

RAIN

[ame]

**SUN,
DAY**

[hi]

**MOON,
MONTH**

[tsuki]

EVENING, DUSK

[yū]

two moons

MANY

[ō-i]

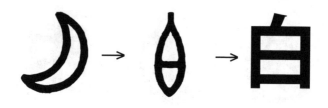

shining moon

WHITE
[shiro]

NOON
[hiru]

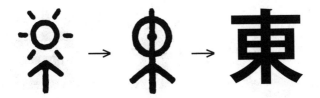

rising sun

EAST
[higashi]

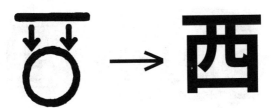

sun under the
horizon

WEST
[nishi]

23

**LIGHT,
RAY**

[hikari]

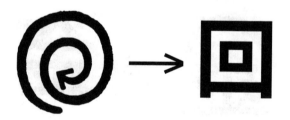

**ROTATE,
TURN**

[mawa-ru]

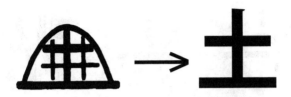

mound

SOIL

[tsuchi]

a mountain, soil and nuggets

GOLD, MONEY

[kin]

entrance
of a hut

ENTER

[hai-ru]

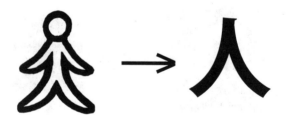

PERSON

[hito]

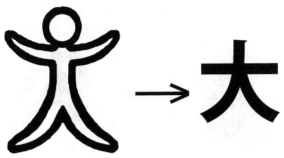

LARGE

[ō-kii]

supported by a
gigantic person (like
Atlas)

**HEAVEN,
SKY**

[ten]

SMALL

[chī-sai]

**LITTLE,
LESS**

[suku-nai]

UP, ABOVE

[ue]

DOWN, BELOW

[shita]

MIDDLE, CENTER

[naka]

balance   **FLAT, PLANE**

[tai-ra]

STOP
[to-maru]

ENGINEERING
[kō]

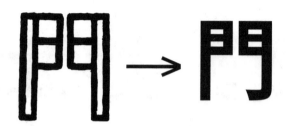

GATE

[mon]

DOOR

[to]

COW
[ushi]

SHEEP
[hitsuji]

DOG

[inu]

ELEPHANT

[zō]

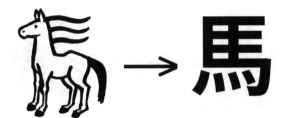

HORSE

[uma]

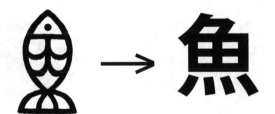

FISH

[sakana]

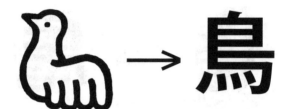

BIRD

[tori]

**WING,
FEATHER**

[hane]

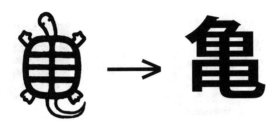

**TURTLE,
TORTOISE**

[kame]

**BUG,
INSECT**

[mushi]

SHELL
[kai]

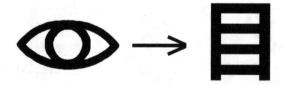

EYE
[me]

EYEBROW

[mayu]

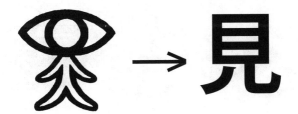

**LOOK,
WATCH**

[mi-ru]

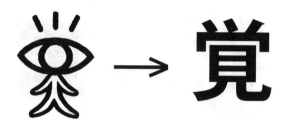

**AWAKE,
REMEMBER**

[obo-eru]

look ahead

**DIRECT,
STRAIGHT**

[choku]

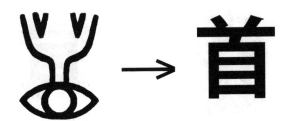

NECK

[kubi]

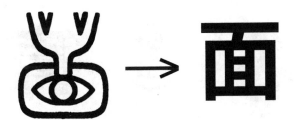

something
surrounding eyes

**FACE,
SURFACE**

[men]

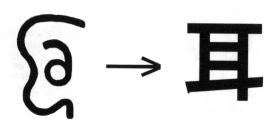

EAR

[mimi]

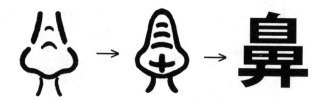

NOSE

[hana]

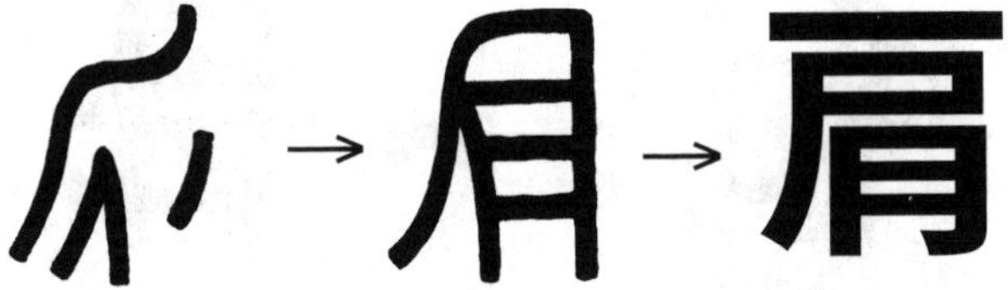

$\nearrow$ → 月 → 肩

SHOULDER

[kata]

$\nwarrow$ → 背 → 背

BACK
(as in body part)

[se]

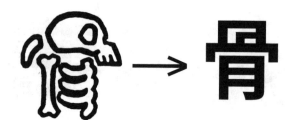

BONE

[hone]

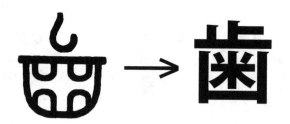

TOOTH

[ha]

44

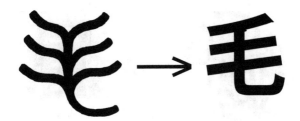

HAIR
[ke]

HAND
[te]

45

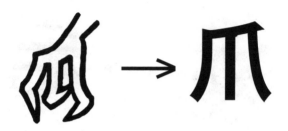

NAIL
[tsume]

HEART
[kokoro]

LEG, FOOT
[ashi]

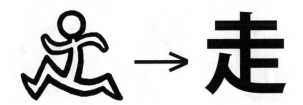

RUN
[hashi-ru]

MOUTH
[kuchi]

TONGUE
[shita]

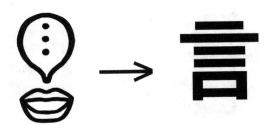

**SAY,
TELL**
[i-u]

SWEET
[ama-i]

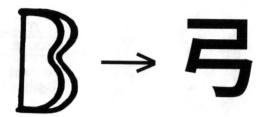

BOW
[yumi]

弓|

PULL
[hi-ku]

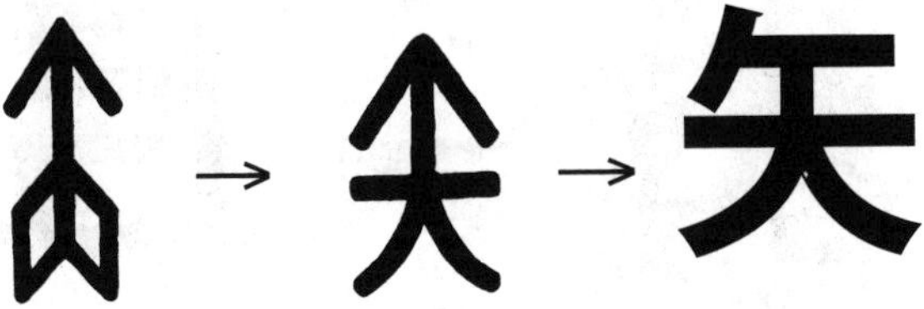

ARROW

[ya]

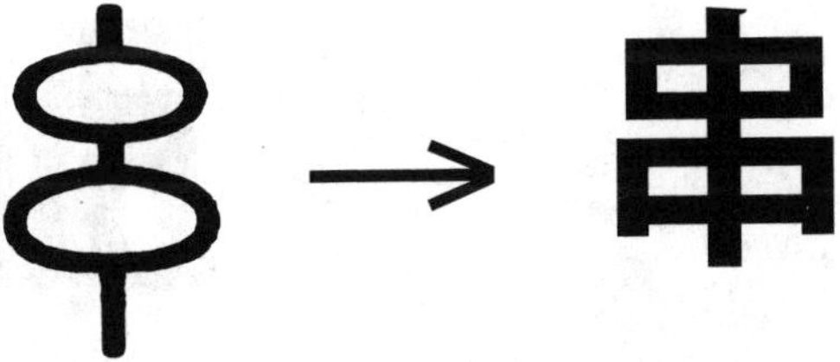

**STICK,
SKEWER**

[kushi]

**PLATE,
DISH**
[sara]

sacrificial

BLOOD
[chi]

**SHIP,
BOAT**
[fune]

SAIL
[ho]

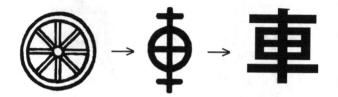

WHEEL, CAR
[kuruma]

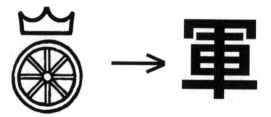

a crown
and a wheel

ARMY
[gun]

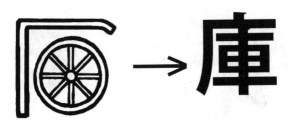

carport

**WAREHOUSE,
STOCK ROOM**

[ko]

BAMBOO

[take]

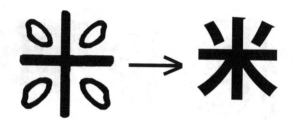

RICE
[kome]

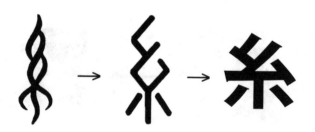

THREAD
[ito]

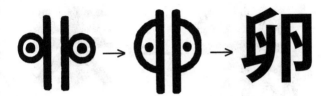

frog spawn
on a stem

EGG
[tamago]

LONG
[naga-i]

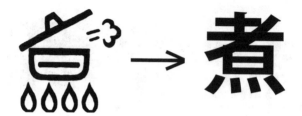

**BOIL,
POACH**
[ni-ru]

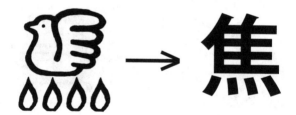

broiler

BURNT
[ko-geru]

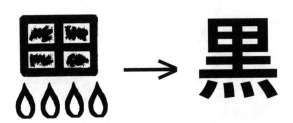

soot

BLACK
[kuro]

RICE FIELD
[ta]

**POINT OUT,
INDICATE**
[shime-su]

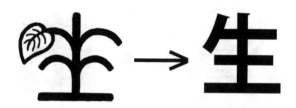

growing plant

**ALIVE,
BORN**
[i-kiru]

60

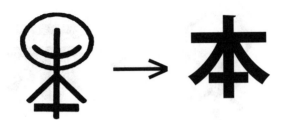

bottom of a tree

**BASE,
ORIGIN**
[hon]

top of a tree

**END,
TERMINAL**
[sue]

61

could not reach
the top

NOT YET
[mi]

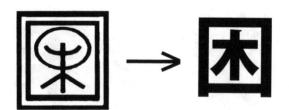

a tree in a box
limited its growth

IN TROUBLE
[koma-ru]

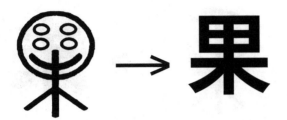

**FRUIT,
RESULT**

[ha-tasu]

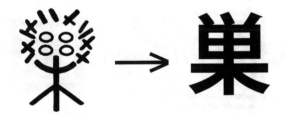

NEST

[su]

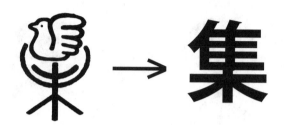

GATHER

[atsu-maru]

**GET ON,
MOUNT**

[no-ru]

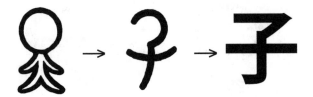

relatively
large head

CHILD

[ko]

a child with an
idea

**LEARN,
STUDY**

[mana-bu]

65

having a
developed skull

**ELDER
BROTHER**

[ani]

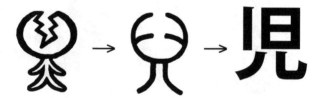

having an
undeveloped skull

**CHILD,
BABY**

[ji]

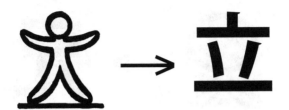

STAND
[ta-tsu]

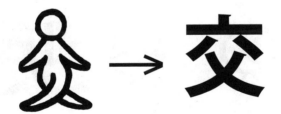

**CROSS,
EXCHANGE**
[maji-waru]

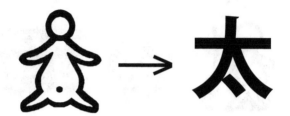

FAT
[futo-i]

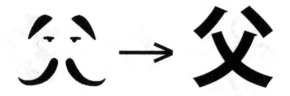

a man with a
grand mustache

FATHER
[chichi]

68

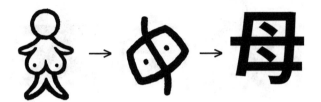

a pregnant
woman having
large breasts

MOTHER

[haha]

FEMALE

[onna]

69

INSIDE

[uchi]

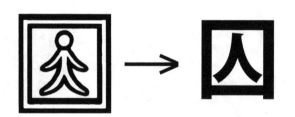

IMPRISONED

[shū]

stand in
between

**INTRODUCE,
INTERMEDIATE**

[kai]

footprint ahead

**AHEAD,
PRIOR TO**

[saki]

debate　　　　　→　　　　COMPETE
　　　　　　　　　　　　　　[kiso-u]

a person
behind a
screen　　　　　→　　　　DEAD,
　　　　　　　　　　　　LOST
　　　　　　　　　　　　[na-i]

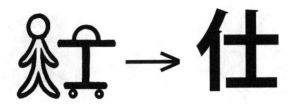

a person and a
dinner wagon

SERVE

[tsuka-eru]

WHAT

[nani]

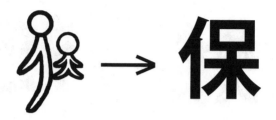

a person carrying a
baby on the back

**TAKE CARE,
MAINTAIN**

[tamo-tsu]

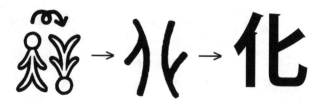

turn over

**CHANGE,
TURN INTO**

[ba-keru]

twins

PAIR
[futa]

**SMILE,
LAUGH**
[wara-u]

season of carnival/
dancing

SUMMER

[natsu]

wind and snow

WINTER

[fuyu]

a lot of "powers"

POWER, MIGHTY

[chikara]

協

COOPERATE

[kyō]

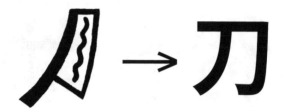

SWORD
[katana]

**EDGE,
BLADE**
[ha]

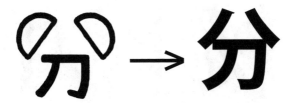

separate with
a sword

**SEPARATE,
MINUTE**
(→separated hour)

[wa-keru]

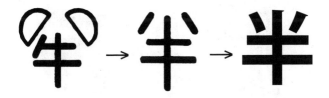

separating
a cow

HALF
[naka-ba]

79

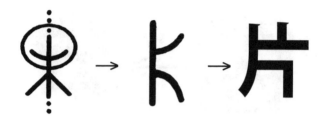

half of a tree

**ONE SIDE,
PIECE**

[kata]

**HATCHET,
AXE**

[kin]

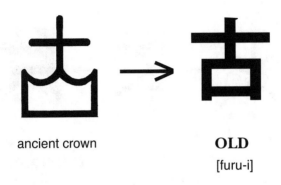

ancient crown

OLD
[furu-i]

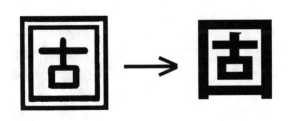

outer surface of an
old thing

**FIRM,
SOLID**
[kata-i]

TOGETHER,
COMMON
[tomo]

attitude during a
face-off

NEGATIVE
[hi]

卝 → 仆 → 行

intersection   **GO**
                                [i-ku]

opinion (→mouth)   **PUBLIC**
made at opened   [ōyake]
space

83

100 → 旧 → 百

HUNDRED
[hyaku]

100 people under
a roof

**INHABIT,
LODGE**
[yado]

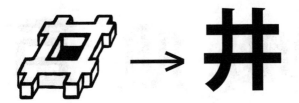

WELL

[i]

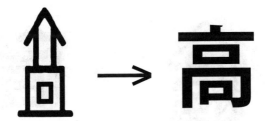

tall building

**HIGH,
TALL**

[taka-i]

a tall building in the
mountains

CAPITAL

[kyō]

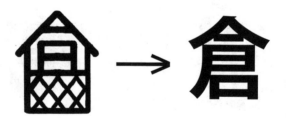

**TREASURE HOUSE,
WAREHOUSE**

[kura]

UMBRELLA
[kasa]

SING, SONG
[uta]

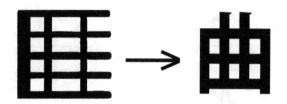

music score → **TUNE**
[kyoku]

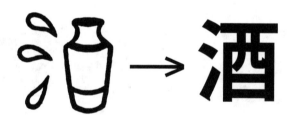

sake container → **ALCOHOL**
[sake]

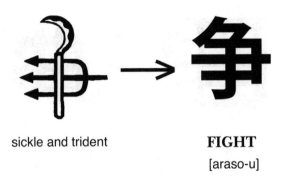

sickle and trident

FIGHT
[araso-u]

SECTION 2

INTEGRATION
of two or more characters

NOTE:

When used as part of another character,

(水 often becomes 氵)

(人 often becomes 亻)

(手 often becomes 扌)

(心 often becomes 忄)

Boldface type in small letters indicates that the translation was introduced in SECTION 1.

Italic type indicates the extended translation, adapted from the original translation in SECTION 1.

Numerals refer to the page on which the character was introduced.

日 + 月 → 明

20   20

sun   **moon**   **BRIGHT**
                                [aka-rui]

日 + 立 + 日 → 暗

20   67   20

stand in front of the **sun**   **DARK**
                                       [kura-i]

日 + 生 → 星

20   60

newly **born sun**, the   **STAR**
seed of a sun   [hoshi]

from the crack in the **gate**,
be able to see the **sun**

BETWEEN
[aida]

put an **ear** on the crack
in the **gate**

**LISTEN,
HEAR**
[ki-ku]

call from the **gate**

**ASK,
QUESTION**
[to-u]

口 + 未 → 味

48   62

food is in one's **mouth**
and has **not yet** reached
one's stomach

TASTE
[aji]

口 + 鳥 → 鳴

48   36

mouth   **bird**

**BIRDSONG,
RINGING**
[na-ku]

口 + 犬 → 吠

48   34

mouth   **dog**

BARK
[ho-eru]

戸 + 犬 → 戻

32   34

our **dog** is at the **door**

**COME BACK,
RETURN**
[modo-ru]

女 + 子 → 好

69   65

the feeling a **woman** has
when taking care of her child

**LIKE,
LOVE**
[su-ku]

女 + 未 → 妹

69   62

new **female** sibling

**YOUNGER
SISTER**
[imōto]

亡 + 女 → 妄
72   69

lose oneself
because of **women**

**FANTASY,
ILLUSION**
[mō]

亡 + 目 → 盲
72   38

lose one's *sight*

BLIND
[mō]

亡 + 心 → 忘
72   46

what one wants to do
when one **loses** one's **heart**

**FORGET,
OBLIVION**
[wasu-reru]

串 + 心 → 患

51　　　46

stab a **stick** into
one's **heart**

SUFFER
[wazura-u]

刃 + 心 → 忍

78　　　46

a **blade** against the
heart

**TOLERATE,
PUT UP WITH**
[shino-bu]

非 + 心 → 悲

82　　　46

negative state
of the **heart**

SAD
[kana-shii]

人 + 非 → 俳

26　　82

a **person** who does
unusual things

PERFORMER
[hai]

人 + 中 → 仲

26　　30

relationship
between **people**

FRIENDSHIP
[naka]

人 + 足 → 促

26　　47

push a **person**
using strong **legs**

**IMPEL,
INDUCE**
[unaga-su]

人 + 言 → 信

26　　49

what one does when
listening to another
person's *words*

**BELIEVE,
TRUST**
[shin-jiru]

人 + 本 → 体

26　　61

basis of a **human** being

BODY
[karada]

人 + 立 → 位

26　　67

where a **person stands**

POSITION
[kurai]

人 + 半 → 伴
26   79

a **person's** better **half**

ACCOMPANY
[tomona-u]

人 + 木 → 休
26   11

a **person** leaning
against a **tree**

REST
[yasu-mu]

木 + 直 → 植
11   40

place a **tree** in
a **straight** position

TO PLANT
[u-eru]

木 + 古 → 枯
11   81

old dying **tree**

WITHER
[ka-reru]

木 + 斤 → 析
11   80

cut a **tree** with an **axe**
and look inside

ANALYZE
[seki]

手 + 斤 → 折
45   80

use an **axe**
with one's **hand**

BREAK,
BEND
[o-ru]

手 + 石 → 拓

45   17

use **hands** to
remove **stones**

PIONEER
[taku]

手 + 軍 → 揮

45   54

use one's **hands**
to control the *troops*

**COMMAND,
CONDUCT**
[ki]

折 + 言 → 誓

102   49

bend one's elbow and
make a statement

SWEAR (as in to
tell the truth)
[chika-u]

言 + 平 → 評
49   30

say something **flat** out

**COMMENT,
CRITICIZE**
[hyō]

言 + 公 → 訟
49   83

say something in **public**

DEBATE (in
court), **SUE**
[shō]

言 + 舌 → 話
49   48

say something using
the **tongue**

**STORY,
TALK**
[hanashi]

水 + 舌 → 活
18   48

water on **tongue**
→talkative

**LIVELY,
VIVID**
[katsu]

水 + 日 + 皿 → 温
18   20   52

water under the **sun** is
evaporating from a **plate**

WARM
[atata-kai]

水 + 中 → 沖
18   30

middle of the sea

OFFSHORE
[oki]

水 + 魚 → 漁

18   35

catch **fish** in the **water**

TO FISH
(as a job)
[ryō]

魚 + 京 → 鯨

35   86

capital fish

WHALE
[kujira]

魚 + 羊 → 鮮

35   33

fish and *meat* at stores
should be...

FRESH
[sen]

羊 + 大 → 美

33   27

large, fat, and rich **sheep**

BEAUTIFUL
[utsuku-shii]

山 + 灰 → 炭

14   13

mountain   **ash**

COAL
[sumi]

丘 + 山 → 岳

16   14

hill   **mountain**

HIGH
MOUNTAIN
[take]

山 + 石 → 岩

14   17

mountain   stone   **ROCK**
[iwa]

石 + 少 → 砂

17   28

stone of **small volume**   **SAND**
[suna]

少 + 力 → 劣

28   77

less   power   **INFERIOR**
[oto-ru]

田 + 力 → 男

59   77

the **power**
of the **rice field**

MALE
[otoko]

火 + 田 → 畑

12   59

dried **rice field**

**VEGETABLE
FIELD**
[hatake]

田 + 介 → 界

59   71

intermediate thing
between **rice fields**

**BORDER,
BORDERED
AREA**
[kai]

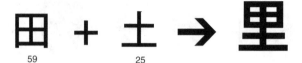

田 + 土 → 里

59 25

rice field and land (→**soil**)

VILLAGE
[sato]

心 + 生 → 性

46 60

a **heart** which a person
has by *nature*

CHARACTER,
PROPERTY
[sei]

牛 + 生 → 牲

33 60

a **living cow** for God

SACRIFICE
[sei]

米 + 分 → 粉

56   79

rice *ground into small pieces*

POWDER
[kona]

分 + 貝 → 貧

79   38

a family *cut* one **clam** into pieces

POOR
[mazu-shii]

白 + 水 → 泉

22   18

where **white** (=fresh) **water** rises

FOUNTAIN
[izumi]

弓 + 長 → 張

50　　　57

a **bow** is pulled **long**

TENSION,
TENSE
[ha-ru]

SECTION 3

COMBINATION
of two or more characters

 **VOLCANO**

ka-zan 12, 14

 **CRATER**

ka-kō 12, 48

 **BLAZE, FLAME**

ka-en 12, 13

 NASAL INFLAMMATION

bi-en 42, 13

 **MOUTH INFLAMMATION, CANKER SORE**

kō-nai-en 48, 70, 13

 **ASHTRAY**

hai-zara 13, 52

 **FIRE** (as in accident)

ka-sai 12, 14

 **MAN-MADE DISASTER**

jin-sai 26, 14

 **NATURAL DISASTER**

ten-sai 27, 14

 **A FIRE BROKEN OUT**

shukka 15, 12

FINDING RELICS FROM THE GROUND

shutsu-do 15, 25

 **PULL A CAR OUT OF A GARAGE**

shukko 15, 55

 (riding a **horse** and **going out** to the battlefield)
↓
RUNNING FOR ELECTION

shutsu-ba 15, 35

 **EXIT**

de-guchi 15, 48

 ENTRANCE

iri-guchi 26, 48

 **BIRTH**

shusshō   15, 60

 CROWD

hito-de   26, 15

 **DUNE**

sa-kyū   108, 16

 **ROCK**

gan-seki   108, 17

 **BROOK, STREAM**

o-gawa   28, 17

 **UPSTREAM**

kawa-kami

 **DOWNSTREAM**

kawa-shimo

 RAINWATER

ama-mizu

 DRIZZLE, LIGHT RAIN

ko-same

 **UNDER WATER**

sui-chū

水車	**WATERWHEEL**
sui-sha	18, 54
水田	**PADDY FIELD**
sui-den	18, 59
氷水	**WATER WITH ICE CUBES, ICE WATER**
kōri-mizu	19, 18
氷山	**ICEBERG**
hyō-zan	19, 14
夕日	**SUNSET**
yū-hi	21, 20

休日	**HOLIDAY**	
kyū-jitsu	101, 20	
日光	**SUNLIGHT**	
nikkō	20, 24	
月光	**MOONLIGHT**	
gekkō	20, 24	
月日	(**months** and **days**) ↓ **THE PASSAGE OF TIME**	
tsuki-hi	20, 20	
多少	**MORE OR LESS**	
ta-shō	21, 28	

 **SWAN**

haku-chō   22, 36

 WHITE PART OF THE EYE

shiro-me   22, 38

 **BLACK PART OF THE EYE**
(dark iris and pupil)

kuro-me   59, 38

 **BLACK-AND-WHITE,
MONOCHROME**

shiro-kuro   22, 59

 PLATINUM

hakkin   22, 25

白昼	**(IN BROAD) DAYLIGHT**
haku-chū	22, 22

白米	**WHITE RICE**
haku-mai	22, 56

明白	**APPARENT**
mei-haku	93, 22

東京	(locating **east** from original Japanese **capital** Kyoto) ↓ **TOKYO**
tō-kyō	23, 86

中東	**MIDDLE EAST**
chū-tō	30, 23

SOIL AND SAND

do-sha   25, 108

 **GOLD DUST**

sa-kin   108, 25

 **A LARGE AMOUNT OF MONEY**

tai-kin   27, 25

 **OBTAIN, AVAILABLE**

nyū-shu   26, 45

 **WHITE PEOPLE**

haku-jin   22, 26

BLACK PEOPLE

koku-jin 59, 26

 **SOLDIER, MILITARY MAN**

gun-jin 54, 26

 **PRISONER**

shū-jin 70, 26

 VISUALLY IMPAIRED

mō-jin 97, 26

 **BEAUTIFUL WOMAN**

bi-jin 107, 26

	**ADULT**	
otona	27, 26	
	**CHILD,** **FAIRY-TALE DWARF**	
ko-bito	28, 26	
	**SIZE**	
dai-shō	27, 28	
	**RAINY WEATHER**	
u-ten	19, 27	
	**UNDER THE BURN-** **ING (SCORCHING)** **SUN**	
en-ten-ka	13, 27, 29	

先天	(nature provided by **heaven prior** to birth) ↓ **INNATE, CONGENITAL**
sen-ten	71, 27

上京	**COME UP TO TOKYO, MOVE TO TOKYO**
jō-kyō	29, 86

炎上	**GO UP IN FLAMES**
en-jō	13, 29

下火	(**down** → decrease) (**fire** → fever) **(a phenomenon) LOSING ITS POPULARITY**
shita-bi	29, 12

下山	**DESCENDING A MOUNTAIN**
ge-zan	29, 14

下見 shita-mi	(**down** → base, background) ↓ **CHECK THE PLACE BEFOREHAND** 29, 39
日中 nicchū	**DAYTIME** 20, 30
水平 sui-hei	(**flat** line of **water**) ↓ **HORIZONTAL** 18, 30
平日 hei-jitsu	(**flat** → nothing special) ↓ **WEEKDAY** 30, 20
平行 hei-kō	(two extending **flat** lines that never cross) ↓ **PARALLEL** 30, 83

 **PAUSE**

chū-shi　　30, 31

 **REST**

kyū-shi　　101, 31

 **WOODWORK, WOODCRAFT**

mokkō　　11, 31

 (great **engineer**)
↓
CARPENTER

dai-ku　　27, 31

 **MAN-MADE, ARTIFICIAL**

jin-kō　　26, 31

入門 nyū-mon 26, 32	(**gate** → entrance of a field) ↓ **INTRODUCTION TO A FIELD OF STUDY**
門出 kado-de 32, 15	(**going out** of the **gate** of one's house) ↓ **STARTING A NEW LIFE**
山羊 ya-gi 14, 33	**GOAT**
金魚 kin-gyo 25, 35	**GOLDFISH**
人魚 nin-gyo 26, 35	**MERMAID**

 | (cannot see at night like **birds**)
↓
NIGHT BLINDNESS

tori-me | 36, 38

 | (a circulating **worm** in one's innards)
↓
ROUNDWORM

kai-chū | 24, 37

 | **CATERPILLAR**

ke-mushi | 45, 37

 | **OTHERS' ATTENTION, PEOPLE'S ATTENTION**

hito-me | 26, 38

 | **SENIOR, SUPERIOR**

me-ue | 38, 29

131

曲目	(**eye** → look → index) ↓ **TITLE OF THE SONG,** **LIST OF THE SONGS**
kyoku-moku	88, 38

眉間	**THE AREA BETWEEN** **ONE'S EYEBROWS** (where you make a frown)
mi-ken	39, 94

見聞	**KNOWLEDGE,** **EXPERIENCE**
ken-bun	39, 94

味見	(**look** → check) ↓ **TRY THE TASTE OF**
aji-mi	95, 39

直行	**GO DIRECT TO,** **NON-STOP**
chokkō	40, 83

 **CONFRONT**

choku-men

 STAND UP STRAIGHT

choku-ritsu

 **SURFACE OF THE MOON**

getsu-men

 **WATER'S SURFACE**

sui-men

 **FLAT SURFACE**

hei-men

NOSTRIL HAIR

hana-ge

 **NOSEBLEED**

hana-ji

 **MUCUS FROM A RUNNING NOSE (SNOT)**

naha-mizu

 BACK (as in body part)

se-naka

 **BACKBONE, SPINE**

se-bone

骨太	(to have **flat bones**) ↓ **STOUT, ROBUST**
hone-buto	44, 68
犬歯	**DOGTOOTH, CANINE TOOTH**
ken-shi	34, 44
	WOOL
yō-mō	33, 45
	**FEATHER, DOWN**
u-mō	36, 45
上手	**SKILLFUL**
jō-zu	29, 45

UNSKILLFUL, CLUMSY, AWKWARD

heta 29, 45

 **UNSKILLFUL SPEAKER, NON-FLUENT**

kuchi-beta 48, 29, 45

 **MAJOR COMPANY IN THE MARKET**

ō-te 27, 45

 **HELPING HAND**

hito-de 26, 45

 **HANDS AND FEET**

te-ashi 45, 47

土足 do-soku	**ENTERING A HOUSE** **WITH ONE'S SHOES ON** 25, 47
足首 ashi-kubi	**ANKLE** 47, 41
小心 shō-shin	**COWARD** 28, 46
下心 shita-gokoro	**SECRET DESIRE,** **ILL-INTENTIONED** 29, 46
男心 otoko-gokoro	**MALE INSTINCTS** 109, 46

 **A WOMAN'S HEART, FEMALE PSYCHOLOGY**

onna-gokoro 69, 46

 **CENTER, HUB, CORE**

chū-shin 30, 46

 **DEEP DOWN, REAL INTENTION**

hon-shin 61, 46

 **PIETY, DEVOTION**

shin-jin 100, 46

 (start of a **thread**)
↓
BEGINNING, CLUE

ito-guchi 56, 48

 **NOT SPICY,
SWEET TASTE (FLAVOR)**

ama-kuchi 49, 48

 EAST EXIT

higashi-guchi 23, 48

 WEST EXIT

nishi-guchi 23, 48

 (mentioning **trivial** things)
↓
**FAULT-FINDING,
SCOLDING**

ko-goto 28, 49

金言 (**golden saying**)
↓
MAXIM

kin-gen 25, 49

明言	**COMMITMENT, DECLARE**
mei-gen	93, 49

弓矢	**BOW-AND-ARROW, ARCHERY**
yumi-ya	50, 51

引火	(**draw** → attract, induce) ↓ **IGNITE, CATCH FIRE**
in-ka	50, 12

出血	**BLEED, HEMORRHAGE**
shukketsu	15, 52

止血	**STOP BLEEDING, HEMOSTASIS**
shi-ketsu	31, 52

 **GET ON A TRAIN,
GET IN A CAR**

jō-sha   64, 54

 **GET OFF A TRAIN,
GET OUT OF A CAR**

ge-sha   29, 54

 **HORSE CARRIAGE**

ba-sha   35, 54

 **CARRY SOMEONE ON
THE SHOULDERS**

kata-guruma   43, 54

歯車 **GEAR**

ha-guruma   44, 54

BODY OF A CAR

sha-tai 54, 100

 INSIDE OF A CAR/TRAIN

sha-nai 54, 70

 **ARMY OF A LARGE NUMBER OF SOLDIERS**

tai-gun 27, 54

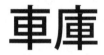 **GARAGE**

sha-ko 54, 55

 **SAFE (for money)**

kin-ko 25, 55

倉庫	**WAREHOUSE**
sō-ko	86, 55

生卵	**RAW EGG**
nama-tamago	60, 57

卵白	**EGG WHITE**
ran-paku	57, 22

首長	**CHIEF, HEADMAN**
shu-chō	41, 57

学長	**HEAD OF A UNIVERSITY/ SCHOOL**
gaku-chō	65, 57

長女	**ELDEST DAUGHTER**	
chō-jo	57, 69	
長男	**ELDEST SON**	
chō-nan	57, 109	
明示	**INDICATE CLEARLY, MANIFEST**	
mei-ji	93, 60	
暗示	**SUGGESTION, IMPLICATION**	
an-ji	93, 60	
生魚	**RAW FISH**	
nama-zakana	60, 35	

学生 gaku-sei	(a person who **lives** mainly by **studying**) ↓ **STUDENT** 65, 60	
大学生 dai-gaku-sei	**UNIVERSITY STUDENT** 27, 65, 60	
中学生 chū-gaku-sei	**JUNIOR-HIGH-SCHOOL STUDENT** 30, 65, 60	
小学生 shō-gaku-sei	**ELEMENTARY-SCHOOL STUDENT** 28, 65, 60	
中高生 chū-kō-sei	**JUNIOR-AND-SENIOR-HIGH-SCHOOL STUDENTS** 30, 85, 60	

先生	(one who was **born** before, supposed to know a lot)
sen-sei	↓ **TEACHER** 71, 60

人生	**LIFE**
jin-sei	26, 60

共生	**SYMBIOSIS**
kyō-sei	82, 60

生活	**LIFE, LIVING**
sei-katsu	60, 105

日本	(seen from China, Japan is located east → **original** place of **sun** rising) **JAPAN**
ni-hon/nippon	20, 61

本日	(**origin** → very thing) ↓ **TODAY**
hon-jitsu	61, 20
本体	**MAIN BODY**
hon-tai	61, 100
本人	**THE PERSON** **HIMSELF/HERSELF**
hon-nin	61, 26
手本	(**origin** → standard) ↓ **EXAMPLE, MODEL**
te-hon	45, 61
見本	**SAMPLE**
mi-hon	39, 61

147

月末	**THE END OF THE MONTH**
getsu-matsu	20, 61
末明	**BEFORE DAWN**
mi-mei	62, 93
未亡人	(a woman whose husband **died** before her) ↓ **WIDOW**
mi-bō-jin	62, 72, 26
卵巣	**OVARY**
ran-sō	57, 63
古巣	**THE PLACE ONE USED TO LIVE OR WORK**
furu-su	81, 63

| 集金 | **COLLECTING MONEY** |
| shū-kin | 64, 25 |

集中	(**gathering** to the **center**)
	↓
	CONCENTRATION
shū-chū	64, 30

| 乗馬 | **HORSE RIDING** |
| jō-ba | 64, 35 |

| 女子 | **FEMALE**
(especially referring to student) |
| jo-shi | 69, 65 |

| 男子 | **MALE**
(especially referring to student) |
| dan-shi | 109, 65 |

| 黒子 | (little **black** spot) ↓ **MOLE** |
| hokuro | 59, 65 |

| 大学 | **UNIVERSITY** |
| dai-gaku | 27, 65 |

| 中学 | **JUNIOR HIGH SCHOOL** |
| chū-gaku | 30, 65 |

| 小学 | **ELEMENTARY SCHOOL** |
| shō-gaku | 28, 65 |

| 入学 | **ENTERING A SCHOOL, SCHOOL ENROLLMENT** |
| nyū-gaku | 26, 65 |

TEMPORARY ABSENCE FROM SCHOOL

kyū-gaku   101, 65

 FIELD TRIP

ken-gaku   39, 65

 **DEGREE** (e.g. Ph. D.)

gaku-i   65, 100

 **STUDY, BRANCH OF STUDY**

gaku-mon   65, 94

 ON CAMPUS

gaku-nai   65, 70

光学	**OPTICS**	
kō-gaku	24, 65	
小児	**CHILD, INFANT, PEDIATRICS** (at a hospital)	
shō-ni	28, 66	
女児	**GIRL**	
jo-ji	69, 66	
男児	**BOY**	
dan-ji	109, 66	
木立	**GROVE**	
ko-dachi	11, 67	

SHOWER THAT FALLS IN THE EVENING

yū-dachi   21, 67

 (**stand** in the **middle**)
↓
NEUTRAL (as in war)

chū-ritsu   30, 67

 **PARENTS**

fu-bo   68, 69

 **MOTHER AND CHILD**

bo-shi   69, 65

 **MOTHER'S BODY**

bo-tai   69, 100

生母	**BIOLOGICAL MOTHER**
sei-bo	60, 69

少女	**LITTLE GIRL**
shō-jo	28, 69

内面	**INSIDE, MENTAL ASPECT**
nai-men	70, 41

内心	**IN ONE'S TRUE HEART, INWARDLY**
nai-shin	70, 46

介入	**INTERVENTION**
kai-nyū	71, 26

仲介	**MEDIATION, INTERMEDIATION**
chū-kai	99, 71

仲介人	**BROKER**
chū-kai-nin	99, 71, 26

先人	**FORERUNNER, PREDECESSOR**
sen-jin	71, 26

先日	(prior day) ↓ **THE OTHER DAY**
sen-jitsu	71, 20

先月	**LAST MONTH**
sen-getsu	71, 20

先見

FORESIGHT

sen-ken   71, 39

先手

THE FIRST MOVE

sen-te   71, 45

手先

(**ahead** → tip, top)
↓
FINGERS, THE USE OF FINGERS

te-saki   45, 71

口先

SUPERFICIAL WORDS

kuchi-saki   48, 71

舌先

THE TIP OF THE TONGUE

shita-saki   48, 71

| 爪先 | **TIPTOE** |
| tsuma-saki | 46, 71 |

| 目先 | **IMMEDIATE FUTURE** |
| me-saki | 38, 71 |

| 行先 | **DESTINATION** |
| yuki-saki | 83, 71 |

| 競走 | **RUNNING RACE** |
| kyō-sō | 72, 47 |

| 競馬 | **HORSE RACING** |
| kei-ba | 72, 35 |

WHAT MONTH?

nan-gatsu 73, 20

 WHAT DAY?
HOW MANY DAYS?

nan-nichi 73, 20

 **WHAT TIME?**
HOW MANY MINUTES?

nan-fun/pun 73, 79

 **HOW MANY PEOPLE?**

nan-nin 73, 26

 **HOW MANY TIMES?**

nan-kai 73, 24

保母 **NURSERY SCHOOL TEACHER**

ho-bo 74, 69

化学 **CHEMISTRY**

ka-gaku 74, 65

生化学 **BIOCHEMISTRY**

sei-ka-gaku 60, 74, 65

化石 **FOSSIL**

ka-seki 74, 17

分化 **DIFFERENTIATION, SPECIALIZATION**

bun-ka 79, 74

少子化	DECREASE IN THE NUMBER OF CHILDREN DUE TO LOW BIRTHRATE
shō-shi-ka	28, 65, 74

双子	TWINS
futa-go	75, 65

火力	HEAT OF THE STOVE, THERMAL POWER
ka-ryoku	12, 77

人力	MANPOWER
jin-riki/ryoku	26, 77

馬力	HORSEPOWER
ba-riki	35, 77

体力	**PHYSICAL STRENGTH**
tai-ryoku	100, 77
引力	**ATTRACTION, GRAVITY**
in-ryoku	50, 77
非力	**INCOMPETENT**
hi-riki	82, 77
学力	**ACADEMIC ACHIEVEMENT**
gaku-ryoku	65, 77
力学	**DYNAMICS, MECHANICS**
riki-gaku	77, 65

| 協力 | **COOPERATION** |
| kyō-ryoku | 77, 77 |

| 活力 | **VITALITY** |
| katsu-ryoku | 105, 77 |

| 力走 | **POWERFUL RUNNING, SPURT** |
| riki-sō | 77, 47 |

| 小刀 | **SMALL KNIFE** |
| ko-gatana | 28, 78 |

| 水分 | **MOISTURE** |
| sui-bun | 18, 79 |

分析 **ANALYSIS**

bun-seki 79, 102

分子 **MOLECULE,
NUMERATOR**

bun-shi 79, 65

分母 **DENOMINATOR**

bun-bo 79, 69

半日 **HALF DAY**

han-nichi 79, 20

半月 **HALF A MONTH**

han-tsuki 79, 20

半生	**HALF ONE'S LIFE, ONE'S LIFE UP TO THIS DAY**
han-sei	79, 60

半面	**ONE SIDE OF AN EVENT, THE OTHER SIDE**
han-men	79, 41

大半	**MORE THAN HALF, MOST PART**
tai-han	27, 79

片目	**ONE-EYED, LOOK WITH ONE EYE**
kata-me	80, 38

片手	**ONE-HANDED**
kata-te	80, 45

 **片言**

(**piece** → incomplete)
↓
BABBLING

kata-koto   80, 49

 木片

**WOOD CHIP,
WOOD BLOCK**

moku-hen   11, 80

 **古米**

OLD RICE

ko-mai   81, 56

 古本

(**origin** → source of knowledge
→ book)
**USED BOOK,
SECONDHAND BOOK**

furu-hon   81, 61

中古

(**middle** → somewhat)
↓
USED, SECONDHAND

chū-ko   30, 81

中古車	**USED CAR**
chū-ko-sha	30, 81, 54

血行	**BLOOD CIRCULATION**
kekkō	52, 83

非行	(**go** → activity) ↓ **DELINQUENCY**
hi-kō	82, 83

行間	(**go** → a line of a book page) ↓ **SPACE BETWEEN LINES, (READ) BETWEEN LINES**
gyō-kan	83, 94

公立	**PUBLICITY FOUNDED** (e.g. public school, public library)
kō-ritsu	83, 67

公平 FAIR

kō-hei   83, 30

公言 DECLARE, PROFESS

kō-gen   83, 49

公示 PUBLIC ANNOUNCEMENT

kō-ji   83, 60

公共 PUBLIC
(e.g. public facility, public
service)

kō-kyō   83, 82

天井 (wooden house frame in the
shape of **well**)
↓
CEILING

ten-jō   27, 85

PARASOL, SUNSHADE

hi-gasa　　　　　20, 87

 **UNDER THE INFLUENCE OF** (as in small companies under a large capital)

san-ka　　　　　87, 29

 **SINGER**

ka-shu　　　　　87, 45

日本酒 **JAPANESE SAKE (RICE WINE)**

ni-hon-shu　　　　　20, 61, 88

 **COMPETITION**

kyō-sō　　　　　72, 89

明日 asu/ashita	(**bright** → new) ↓ **TOMORROW** 93, 20
明暗 mei-an	**LIGHT AND DARKNESS,** **FORTUNATE AND** **UNFORTUNATE** 93, 93
暗黒 an-koku	**DARKNESS** (as in era, town) 93, 59
火星 ka-sei	**MARS** 12, 93
水星 sui-sei	**MERCURY** 18, 93

木星	**JUPITER**
moku-sei	11, 93

金星	**VENUS**
kin-sei	25, 93

土星	**SATURN**
do-sei	25, 93

火星人	**MARTIAN**
ka-sei-jin	12, 93, 26

谷間	**GORGE, VALLEY**
tani-ma	16, 94

IN BETWEEN, INTERMEDIATE

chū-kan 30, 94

 FRIEND, COMRADE

naka-ma 99, 94

 **DAYTIME**

hiru-ma 22, 94

 **HUMAN BEING**

nin-gen 26, 94

 **MONOTONOUS FLAVOR, TASTELESS**

ō-aji 27, 95

| 甘味 | SWEET TASTE |
| kan-mi | 49, 95 |

| 人間味 | HUMAN TOUCH, HUMANE |
| nin-gen-mi | 26, 94, 95 |

| 共鳴 | RESONANCE, SYMPATHY |
| kyō-mei | 82, 95 |

| 悲鳴 | SCREAM, SHRIEK |
| hi-mei | 98, 95 |

| 好評 | FAVORABLE COMMENT, GOOD REPUTATION |
| kō-hyō | 96, 104 |

PERSON WHO LIVES MAKING "HAIKU," POET

hai-jin   99, 26

 **MATCHMAKER (OF MARRIAGES)**

nakōdo   99, 26

 JOIN A RELIGIOUS SECT

nyū-shin   26, 100

 **BLIND BELIEF**

mō-shin   97, 100

人体 **HUMAN BODY**

jin-tai   26, 100

上体	**UPPER BODY**
jō-tai	29, 100
体内	**INTERNAL BODY**
tai-nai	100, 70
天体	**HEAVENLY BODY, CELESTIAL BODY**
ten-tai	27, 100
固体	**SOLID BODY**
ko-tai	81, 100
水位	**WATER LEVEL**
sui-i	18, 100

| 上位 | **HIGHER RANK, SUPERIOR** |
| jō-i | 29, 100 |

| 下位 | **LOWER RANK, INFERIOR** |
| ka-i | 29, 100 |

| 首位 | **HEAD POSITION, FIRST PLACE** |
| shu-i | 41, 100 |

| 植木 | **TREE PLANTED IN THE GARDEN** |
| ue-ki | 101, 11 |

| 植林 | **AFFORESTATION** |
| shoku-rin | 101, 11 |

植毛	**HAIR IMPLANT**	
shoku-mō	101, 45	
田植	**RICE-PLANTING**	
ta-ue	59, 101	
入植	("planting" people → colony) **IMMIGRATION INTO A COLONY**	
nyū-shoku	26, 101	
枯木	**DEAD TREE**	
kare-ki	102, 11	
折半	**DIVIDE INTO TWO HALVES, GO FIFTY-FIFTY**	
seppan	102, 79	

HAND LANGUAGE, SIGN LANGUAGE

shu-wa   45, 104

 SHORT STORY

ko-banashi   28, 104

 LONG TALK

naga-banashi   57, 104

 (**warm** → degree of warmth → temperature)
↓
HIGH TEMPERATURE

kō-on   85, 105

体温 **BODY TEMPERATURE**

tai-on   100, 105

保温	MAINTAIN A CERTAIN TEMPERATURE, KEEP WARM
ho-on	74, 105

水温	WATER TEMPERATURE
sui-on	18, 105

温水	WARM WATER
on-sui	105, 18

温泉	HOT SPRING, SPA
on-sen	105, 111

大漁	CATCH A LARGE AMOUNT OF FISH
tai-ryō	27, 106

鮮魚	**FRESH FISH**
sen-gyo	106, 35

鮮血	**FRESH BLOOD**
sen-ketsu	106, 52

鮮明	**(VISUALLY) VIVID**
sen-mei	106, 93

美女	**BEAUTIFUL WOMAN**
bi-jo	107, 69

美男	**HANDSOME MAN**
bi-nan	107, 109

美化	BEAUTIFY, GLORIFY
bi-ka	107, 74

美学	AESTHETIC
bi-gaku	107, 65

木炭	CHARCOAL
moku-tan	11, 107

石炭	COAL
seki-tan	17, 107

石灰	LIME
sekkai	17, 13

山岳	**MOUNTAINS, ALPINE**	
san-gaku	14, 107	
下劣	**VULGAR, MEAN** (person)	
ge-retsu	29, 108	
劣化	**DETERIORATION**	
rekka	108, 74	
大男	**LARGE MAN, GIANT**	
ō-otoko	27, 109	
男女	**MAN AND WOMAN**	
dan-jo	109, 69	

| 田畑 | **RICE FIELD AND VEGETABLE FIELD, FIELDS FOR AGRICULTURE** |
| ta-hata | 59, 109 |

| 母性 | **MOTHERHOOD, MATERNITY** |
| bo-sei | 69, 110 |

| 天性 | (**property** given by **heaven**) ↓ **APTITUDE, NATURE** |
| ten-sei | 27, 110 |

| 本性 | (**original** → true) ↓ **ONE'S TRUE CHARACTER** |
| hon-shō | 61, 110 |

| 水性 | **WATER-SOLUBLE** |
| sui-sei | 18, 110 |

中性	**NEUTRAL** (neither acid nor alkali)
chū-sei	30, 110

女性	**FEMALE**
jo-sei	69, 110

男性	**MALE**
dan-sei	109, 110

貧血	**ANEMIA**
hin-ketsu	111, 52

活性化	**ACTIVATE**
kassei-ka	105, 110, 74

 **POVERTY**

hin-kon   111, 62

APPENDIX

1. Keys to further study

短	short	内	inside	高	high
長	long	外	outside	低	low

北
north

西
west

東
east

南
south

春
spring

冬
winter

夏
summer

秋
fall

母	mother	姉	elder sister	妹	younger sister
父	father	兄	elder brother	弟	younger brother

2. Keys to further study—numbers

1	一	**11**	十一
2	二	**12**	十二
3	三	**20**	二十
4	四	**100**	百
5	五	**101**	百一
6	六	**110**	百十
7	七	**200**	二百
8	八	**1,000**	一千
9	九	**10,000**	一万
10	十		

INDEX

In this index, the characters are arranged simply by the number of lines in the character, not by the number of actual strokes. For example, 口 (mouth) is categorized in "4 lines" in this index, but it is written with 3 strokes in proper orthography.

190

❏ **6 LINES** ❏

❏ **16 AND MORE LINES** ❏

BIBLIOGRAPHY

Shinjigen 232nd edition. Kadokawashoten, 1985, Tokyo.

New Little Japanese-English Dictionary 5th edition. Kenkyusha, 1987, Tokyo.

Romaji Japanese-English Dictionary. Sanseido, 2000, Tokyo.

English-Japanese Dictionary for the General Reader. Kenkyusha,1984, Tokyo.

NOTES

NOTES